NEW VANGUARD 208

US NAVY DREADNOUGHTS 1914–45

RYAN K. NOPPEN

First published in Great Britain in 2014 by Osprey Publishing,
PO Box 883, Oxford, OX1 9PL, UK
1385 Broadway, 5th Floor, New York, NY 10018, USA
E-mail: info@ospreypublishing.com

Osprey Publishing is part of Bloomsbury Publishing Plc

A CIP catalog record for this book is available from the British Library

Print ISBN: 978 1 78200 386 1
PDF ebook ISBN: 978 1 78200 387 8
ePub ebook ISBN: 978 1 78200 388 5

Index by Fionbar Lyons
Typeset in Sabon and Myriad Pro
Originated by PDQ Media, Bungay, UK
Printed in China through Worldprint Ltd

17 18   10 9 8 7 6 5 4

Osprey Publishing is supporting the Woodland Trust, the UK's leading
woodland conservation charity, by funding the dedication of trees.

www.ospreypublishing.com

ACKNOWLEDGMENTS

The author wishes to thank the following individuals for their assistance
with this project: Winnie Trippet and Travis Davis of the Battleship *Texas*
State Historic Site, James A. Knechtmann and Lisa Crunk of the Naval
History & Heritage Command, Michael Mohl of navsource.org, and finally
James Lee of Deepscape Photography.

DEDICATION

This book is dedicated to Frank Bussema, crew member of USS *Texas*
(1914–1916), veteran of the 1914 Veracruz Expedition, veteran of the First
World War, and Great-Great Uncle of the author.

CONTENTS

US NAVY DREADNOUGHTS 1914–45

INTRODUCTION

The United States was the second of the great naval powers to embrace the concept of the all-big-gun dreadnought battleship in the early 20th century. The US Navy was seen as an upstart by much of the international community, after it experienced a rapid increase in strength in the wake of the Spanish-American War. American naval expansion paralleled that of another upstart naval power, Germany, whose navy also saw meteoric growth in this period. What is little known is that a tacit naval arms race developed in the late 19th and early 20th centuries between these two powers, due primarily to soured foreign relations caused by a rivalry over colonial territory in the Pacific and an economic rivalry in Latin America. Matters were not helped by the fact that these two economic and recently expansionist powers were led by strong-willed and ambitious men: Kaiser Wilhelm II and President Theodore Roosevelt, both of whom were looking for an international "place in the sun" for their respective nations. The Kaiser envisioned Germany's "place in the sun" in the Far East and in the "economic" colonization of Latin America. Roosevelt sought to defend America's "place in the sun," which he saw as comprising the recently acquired Philippine archipelago, defending his Open Door policy in China, and protecting America's "sacred" Monroe Doctrine, which protected the United States' traditional sphere of influence in Latin America. The bombastic oratory of both leaders combined with a number of diplomatic faux pas (particularly Admiral George Dewey's standoff with Admiral Otto von Diederichs in Manila Bay in 1898 and the Venezuelan Crisis of 1902) led the naval planners of both nations to prepare contingency war plans against each other. Ironically, both sides believed that this would be a conflict exclusively between each other. The Kaiser's government believed Great Britain and the rest of Europe would remain neutral given Europe's generally negative reaction to America's war against Spain; the same opinion was shared in Washington DC.

Between 1897 and 1903, German naval planners researched a number of scenarios regarding a naval war with the United States, the culmination of which was a highly detailed war plan known as Operations Plan III. This plan and all other thoughts of fighting a naval war with the United States were abruptly set aside however in 1904 and completely shelved by 1906, after the formation of the Entente Cordiale between Britain and France forced a radical change in the foreign policy priorities of the Kaiser's government. In 1903, the United States Navy General Board, headed by Admiral Dewey, began to draw up contingency operational plans for a potential naval conflict in the Caribbean with Germany, culminating into what would eventually be known as War Plan Black. Berlin may have abandoned its colonial ambitions in the western hemisphere, but this did not mean that the United States was aware of this development. Instead the US Navy intensified its planning for an isolated naval war with Germany between 1904 and 1913. This period of anti-German contingency planning coincided with the debut in 1906 of a revolutionary naval weapons platform, the all-big-gun HMS *Dreadnought*. With more battleships needed to meet the requirements of War Plan Black, this was a development that could not be ignored.

Admiral Prinz Heinrich von Preußen, brother of Kaiser Wilhelm II, with President Theodore Roosevelt during the prince's visit to America in 1902. German and American rivalry for influence in Asia and Latin American led to the development of the US Navy's dreadnought program. (Library of Congress LC-DIG-stereo-1s01923)

Theodore Roosevelt was aware of the idea of an all-big-gun battleship as early as 1902, when he received conceptual plans for a battleship armed with a primary battery of 12 heavy guns and a tertiary battery of light quick-firing guns, designed by Lieutenant Commander Homer Poundstone. Roosevelt praised Poundstone's design, but doubted he could get approval from the Navy department and Congress for such a revolutionary ship. Poundstone's design also caught the attention of Lieutenant Commander William S. Sims, an up-and-coming naval officer, who closely followed modern warship developments and tactics in Europe. In September 1902, Lieutenant Sims was made Inspector of the Target Practice for the Atlantic Squadron. From gunnery practices, Sims came to the conclusion that effective targeting aboard ships with a highly mixed armament was difficult as the splashes from 12-inch, 10-inch and 8-inch shells were virtually indistinguishable, which further strengthened the argument in favor of a single-caliber primary armament. Events taking place halfway around the world in 1905 seemed to confirm Sims's belief that a ship bearing uniform large-caliber primary guns would give a battle fleet a major advantage in future combat. On May 27–28, 1905, the Japanese Combined Fleet of Admiral Togo Heihachiro soundly defeated the Russian Baltic Fleet at the battle of Tsushima. Foreign observers noted that the well-trained Japanese gunners, aboard battleships equipped with modern Barr & Stroud range-finders, scored accurate and crippling hits on the Russian warships with 12-inch guns firing at a range of around 8 miles. The damage and confusion aboard the Russian ships caused by the accurate bombardment from long-range then presented Togo with the opportunity to deploy his destroyers and torpedo boats in a series of torpedo attacks that could not be effectively opposed. In the summer of 1904, the US General Board requested the Naval War College conduct a hypothetical study to determine the effectiveness of future torpedoes, with an estimated range of

Lieutenant Commander William S. Sims, who served as a naval advisor to Theodore Roosevelt, was an early proponent of the all-big-gun battleship. He is shown here in 1919 as a vice-admiral after commanding US naval forces in Europe in World War I. Behind him is Assistant Secretary of the Navy Franklin D. Roosevelt. (Library of Congress, LC-DIG-hec-11935)

7,000 to 8,000 yards. Traditionally, the effective range of battle was dictated by the effective range of torpedoes. The results of Tsushima answered the General Board's inquiry: accurate gunnery had taken place at a range of over 14,000 yards. The torpedo was no longer the primary threat to a battleship rather the heavy gun as a warship could be damaged or sunk well before it came into range to fire its torpedoes. If future combat was to follow the precedent of Tsushima, then any ensuing battles would be decided by long-range heavy guns. However, it was the British Royal Navy that finally forced the issue of the all-big-gun battleship, when details about HMS *Dreadnought*'s design became known to the US Navy in the summer of 1905. When reports of Tsushima reached the Admiralty, the results of the battle confirmed the strategic vision of Admiral John "Jackie" Fisher's plans for an all-big-gun battleship and HMS *Dreadnought* was laid down on October 2, 1905. With the construction of a single ship, the Royal Navy rendered all previous battleships more or less obsolete.

Analyses of the battle of Tsushima seemed to vindicate American supporters of the dreadnought battleship, but it also threw an unexpected wrench into strategic naval planning. With the Czar's navy nearly obliterated and the British in an alliance with Japan, there was no counterweight to potential Japanese naval and territorial expansion in the Pacific. Japanese anger at American meddling in the Treaty of Portsmouth, which ended the Russo-Japanese War, and anti-Japanese immigration measures on the American West Coast heightened tensions between the two nations. Diplomatic agreements helped to return relations to an even keel and the celebrated 1907–09 cruise of the Great White Fleet, a perfect example of Roosevelt's "speak softly and carry a big stick" approach to diplomacy, intentionally intimidated the Japanese away from pursuing any expansionist moves. Nevertheless, the specter of Japanese naval expansion began to haunt American naval planners and by 1906 contingency plans for war with Japan had already begun to take shape, the first of which to be formally adopted, in 1911, being the first version of Plan Orange. At this time Japan was considered a secondary threat to Germany, primarily because of Japan's limited industrial capacity and inexperience in building large capital ships. Nevertheless, American admirals demanded that all new capital ships must have sufficient range to operate deep in the Pacific, in the event of conflict with Japan. Thus it was that the initial period of American dreadnought construction, from 1906 to 1910, began against the backdrop of a perceived major German naval threat in the Caribbean and a perceived minor Japanese naval threat in the Pacific. Reluctance among some anti-imperialist members of the US Congress to fund a new naval weapons platform (especially when a large fleet of pre-dreadnoughts was in the final stages of completion) made it difficult for the US Navy to keep pace with German dreadnought construction during this period. Furthermore, the dreadnoughts that were constructed between 1906 and 1911 were all experimental in nature; the first American dreadnought laid down was not commissioned until six months before the fifth class of dreadnoughts was approved. This meant that some of the ships had design problems or teething issues due to untested equipment or machinery. At the time, however, the need for more ships outweighed the time required to fully test new design theories and equipment. Of course, one must also take into account the fact that in the early years of the twentieth century new naval technologies were being developed at a rapid pace and that all naval powers risked flaws in their early dreadnought designs rather than fall behind their potential rivals. In a sense, the first five classes of American dreadnoughts can be termed as the "experimental classes," as several different design approaches were taken with them and the lessons learned from their design, construction and trials heavily influenced the carefully planned and rather homogenous "all-or-nothing" five classes of American super-dreadnoughts that followed. This book examines the development, characteristics and service of these first five classes of American dreadnought battleships.

The forward 12-inch turrets on *Michigan*. The bridge platform is located within the caged foremast behind the canvas, while the conning tower is just fore of and below the bridge platform. Designers wanted dreadnought captains to operate their ships from within the conning towers rather than flying bridges, hence the bare upper works of American dreadnoughts. (Library of Congress, LC-DIG-ggbain-07958)

THE SOUTH CAROLINA CLASS

By the summer of 1903 there had been enough discussion and theorizing about the potential of an all-big-gun battleship in domestic naval circles that in October the Navy General Board requested a feasibility study from the Navy Bureau of Construction and Repair for an all-big-gun battleship mounting up to twelve 12-inch guns. The architects within the bureau had little interest in this enterprise, initially believing it to be unfeasible, and obstinately refused to begin a project that might render their previous designs, and that of the Connecticut class which they were still completing, virtually obsolete. By 1905, the Bureau of Construction and Repair still had not begun serious design studies. President Roosevelt intervened personally and made it clear to the bureau that he wanted designs for an all-big-gun battleship. With the urging of both the President and the Navy General Board, Congress authorized the construction of two new battleships, the South Carolina class, with the heaviest possible armor and armament within a maximum 16,000-ton normal displacement on March 3, 1905.

While American designs for an all-big-gun battleship preceded those of HMS *Dreadnought*, a series of bureaucratic obstacles prevented the US Navy from launching the world's first warship of this kind. The most serious of these was the congressional weight restriction for the new South Carolina

"No Limit" is the title of this 1909 cartoon taken from the contemporary satire magazine *Puck*. It accurately reflects the fact that by this time the United States was a dedicated participant in the worldwide high-stakes naval arms race. (Library of Congress LC-DIG-ppmsca-26411)

class battleships to 16,000 tons, which was seemingly not sufficient to accommodate a reasonably fast, well-protected ship mounting at least eight 12-inch guns. Rear-Admiral Washington Capps, the Constructor of the Navy and Chief of the Bureau of Construction and Repair, sought to solve this problem by designing a battleship with centerline superfiring turrets; in other words, all gun turrets would be located along the longitudinal center (centerline) of the ship. Two of the ship's four turrets positioned partially above the other two reduced the length of the ship, thus saving weight, while forsaking wing turrets eliminated the need for heavy internal structural support to bear the combined weight of two turrets (used on *Dreadnought* and pre-dreadnought designs) located at the same position along the centerline. Perhaps more strategically important than weight reduction, at least in terms of future battleship construction, was that the centerline superfiring arrangement allowed the ship to bring all of its primary guns to bear when firing a broadside. This gave Capps's South Carolina class broadside firepower equal to that of *Dreadnought*, even though the latter possessed two more 12-inch guns. As the most efficient use of area and weight, Capps's centerline superfiring design would eventually become the international standard of battleship primary gun turret arrangement.

The obsession with weight-saving measures also resulted in a distinctively American dreadnought design feature: the caged mast. Dreadnoughts of the Royal Navy used a heavy, armored tripod mast to support the observer's platform. Capps believed that such a mast took up too much weight and could all too easily be knocked out by a direct hit, essentially blinding the ship's primary guns. The solution he offered was a caged mast, a tall cylindrical structure constructed from a lattice netting of steel strips. While very lightweight, the interwoven steel strips created a strong and sturdy structure that would remain intact even after absorbing battle damage. Firing tests confirmed the strength of the masts and they were installed on the South Carolinas, as well as fitted retroactively to the navy's pre-dreadnoughts. With the observation platform 100 feet above the waterline, the caged masts allowed observers to spot targets up to 10,000 yards away. The armor plate that provided protection for the individual ships of the South Carolinas and the next four classes of American dreadnoughts did not come from a single source but rather was a patchwork of plate from three companies: Carnegie Steel Corporation, Bethlehem Steel Corporation and Midvale Steel Company. Carnegie Steel produced a variant of Krupp cemented steel plate. Bethlehem and Midvale, not wanting to pay licensing fees to Krupp, each developed forms of face-hardened chromium-nickel-steel armor known as non-cemented plate. Tests later showed that the Bethlehem and Midvale

non-cemented plates were more brittle than Krupp cemented plate, but by that point non-cemented plates had already been utilized in all dreadnoughts laid down before 1913.

Although the South Carolina class battleships were authorized in March 1905, final specifications were not released to bidders until over a year later. Finally on December 17, 1906, USS *Michigan* (BB-27) was laid down in the yards of the New York Shipbuilding Corporation. USS *South Carolina* (BB-26) was laid down the following day by William Cramp & Sons Shipbuilding Company of Philadelphia. Work on these ships was slow as *Michigan* was not launched until May 26, 1908 and commissioned on January 4, 1910, while *South Carolina* followed on July 11, 1908 and December 15, 1910 respectively.

One of the South Carolina class dreadnoughts in dry dock in the Brooklyn Navy Yard, with a good view of the hull shape of early American dreadnoughts prior to the introduction of torpedo bulges. (Library of Congress, LC-D4-73024)

South Carolina Class Specifications
Dimensions: length: 452 feet 9 inches; beam: 80 feet 5 inches; draft: 24 feet 7 inches
Full displacement: 17,617 tons
Ship's complement: 869 men
Armament: eight 12-inch/45-caliber Mark 5 guns mounted in four twin turrets (USN 12-inch /45 guns had a range at 15° elevation of 20,000 yards, could penetrate $12\frac{1}{5}$ inches of face-hardened Harvey steel plate at 9,000 yards with a 870-pound armor-piercing shell and had an elevation range from -5° to 15°; 100 rounds were carried per gun; two to three rounds could be fired per minute); twenty-two 3-inch/50-caliber antitorpedo-boat

South Carolina sailing past Morro Castle on its way out of Havana harbor in 1910. American dreadnoughts participated in fleet maneuvers off Guantanamo Bay every winter prior to American entry in World War I. (Library of Congress, LC-6a23470u)

guns (USN 3-inch/50 gun had a range at 4.3° elevation of 4,500 yards and an elevation range of -10° to 15°; 300 rounds were carried per gun); two underwater 21-inch torpedo tubes for Bliss-Leavitt 21-inch Mark 3 torpedoes

Machinery: two vertical triple-expansion engines, fired by 12 Babcock & Wilcox boilers producing 16,500 ihp (indicated horsepower) and driving two screws at a maximum speed of 18½ knots

Maximum range: 5,000 nautical miles at 10 knots

Protection: armored belt, 12 inches thick over the main magazines and 11 inches thick over the machinery areas, tapering to 9 inches at both ends; casemate armor: 10 inches, tapering to 8 inches towards the top; conning tower: 12 inches; barbette armor: 10 inches at exposed areas and 8 inches where covered by another barbette; primary turrets: 12-inch armor over faces and sides; deck armor: 2 inches thick over vital areas and 1½ inches thick over the rest.

THE DELAWARE AND FLORIDA CLASSES

Delaware being fitted out, with a good view of the 5-inch/50 gun in the port bow. (Library of Congress, LC-DIG-ggbain-04377)

As details of the plans of HMS *Dreadnought* began to leak out in the summer of 1905, the Navy General Board realized already that the displacement of the planned South Carolina class would not be adequate to accommodate subsequent American battleship designs if they were to keep pace with developments abroad. The General Board requested that maximum normal displacement be raised to 18,000 tons, but Congress refused to support the motion. It was only after *Dreadnought* was launched that Congress realized that the 16,000-ton displacement limit could no longer be realistically supported. What little information about *Dreadnought* there was at the time gave the impression that it was a much superior ship to the South Carolina class design. Although this information later proved to be exaggerated, it caused enough concern among US Navy circles to inspire a major reappraisal of design methodology. This view was reinforced when, on May 17, 1905, the Japanese laid down the *Satsuma*, a semi-dreadnought possessing four 12-inch guns and twelve 10-inch guns, with a displacement of 19,700 tons. If a mixed armament battleship could have a similar displacement to *Dreadnought* (18,100 tons), there was clearly no logic in retaining strict displacement limits, particularly if new American battleships were to effectively rival those of foreign navies.

On June 29, 1906, Congress finally relented and repealed the displacement limit for future ships, authorizing the construction of a new one that same day and a second of the same class on March 2, 1907. Capps and the Bureau of Construction and Repair put forward a design for a new dreadnought battleship mounting ten 12-inch guns. USS *Delaware* (BB-28) was laid down on November 11, 1907 at the Newport News Shipbuilding Company, launched on February 6, 1909 and commissioned on April 4, 1910. Her sister, USS *North Dakota* (BB-29), was laid down on December 16, 1907 at the Fore River Shipbuilding Company, launched on November 10, 1908 and commissioned on April 11, 1910. A major difference between the two Delawares was means of propulsion. *Delaware* was fitted with vertical triple-expansion engines, while *North Dakota* was fitted with new Curtis direct-drive marine turbines, manufactured by the General Electric Company, in order to evaluate this relatively new form of marine propulsion.

On May 13, 1908, Congress authorized the construction of the two Florida class dreadnoughts. The new Florida class ships were near-identical to the Delaware class with a few minor changes. The engine rooms were longer in order to accommodate four Parsons turbines. The British-designed turbines were selected as Parsons had greater experience in turbine construction for warships than Curtis. As *North Dakota*, equipped with Curtis turbines, was still under construction the Navy had not yet been able to evaluate their efficiency at sea and it seemed more prudent to utilize a less-experimental turbine. Other differences from the Delaware class included a rearrangement of the funnels between the two caged masts and long-based rangefinders that were mounted to the tops of Turrets 2, 3 and 4. Furthermore the Florida class was designed with a larger conning tower that could accommodate ship and fire control stations. However, both the Delaware and Florida classes had a fundamental

Admiral Togo leaving *North Dakota* after an inspection during his 1911 visit to the United States. Concern over a growing Japanese naval presence in Asia resulted in requirements for new American dreadnoughts to have the range necessary to operate deep in the Pacific. (Library of Congress, LC-DIG-ggbain-09526)

Sailors aboard *North Dakota* engaged in the miserable and filthy task of coaling. Coal was hoisted aboard in sacks and then shoveled into hatches leading down to the coal bunkers. The decks were then swept and swabbed clean. (Library of Congress, LC-USZ62-137317)

Florida sailing under the Brooklyn Bridge in 1912. (Library of Congress LC-USZ62-100107)

problem regarding the layout of the machinery areas. The placement of the engine room between Turrets 3 and 4 resulted in steam lines running from the boiler rooms amidships around Turret 3's magazine to the engine rooms. There was the potential for the heat from the steam lines to accelerate the breakdown of the gunpowder in the magazine. This arrangement was in part necessitated by the large amount of space required for coal-fired boilers, but it was a design aspect that line officers were never pleased with. USS *Florida* (BB-30) was laid down on March 9, 1909 at the New York Navy Yard, launched on May 12, 1910 and commissioned on September 15, 1911. It was followed swiftly by USS *Utah* (BB-31), which was laid down in the yards of the New York Shipbuilding Corporation on March 15, 1909, launched on December 23, 1909 and commissioned on August 31, 1911.

Delaware Class Specifications
Dimensions: length: 519 feet; beam: 85 feet 4 inches; draft: 27 feet 3 inches
Full displacement: 22,060 tons
Ship's complement: 933 men
Armament: ten 12-inch/45-caliber Mark 5 guns mounted in five twin turrets; fifteen 5-inch/50-caliber guns (USN 5-inch/50 gun could penetrate $1^2/_5$-inch of armor with a 50-pound shell at 9,000 yards, had an elevation range of -10° to 15°; 240 rounds were carried per gun and six to eight rounds could be fired per minute), ten mounted in casemates amidships located below the main deck, two in casemates towards the stern and two in casemates in the bow just forward of Turret 1; two underwater 21-inch torpedo tubes for Bliss-Leavitt 21-inch Mark 3 torpedoes

THE SOUTH CAROLINA CLASS: USS *MICHIGAN*
While the innovative centerline superfiring turret arrangement helped to limit the displacement of the South Carolina class design, additional economizing to keep the design within the 16,000-ton maximum displacement led to mediocre results in other design aspects. Protective armor could not be sacrificed; it was actually increased from that of the Connecticut class of pre-dreadnoughts because of fears of torpedo damage. Designer Washington Capps concluded that the remaining excess weight would have to be removed from the machinery spaces. The small vertical triple-expansion engines combined with a small boiler space resulted in a maximum speed of only 18½ knots, slower than *Dreadnought's* $21^2/_3$ knots. The slow speed of the South Carolina class would later limit the ships' operational deployments.

Overall armament would also suffer as a result of the 16,000-ton displacement limit. As a weight-saving measure, Capps stepped down the afterdeck by one level. Lacking secondary armament, the South Carolina class ships instead mounted twenty-two 3-inch/50-caliber antitorpedo boat tertiary guns. Mounting an effective number of higher-caliber secondary guns would have taken up too much weight, but the higher number of tertiary guns proved to be ineffective. Firing tests showed that the 3-inch/50 gun could penetrate 2 inches of Krupp steel only at a range of 1,000 yards or less, which was not particularly impressive as the latest torpedoes, when mounted on a destroyer or torpedo boat, could be fired from up to a maximum range of 4,000 yards. Shown here is *Michigan* in its World War I paint scheme.

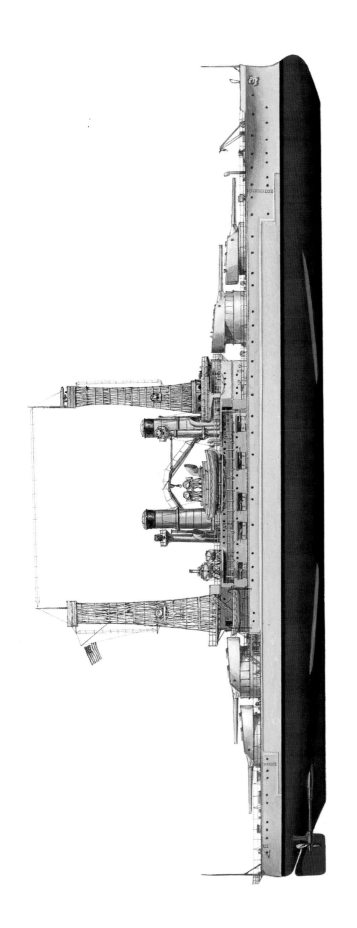

Machinery: *Delaware*: two vertical triple-expansion engines, fired by 14 Babcock & Wilcox boilers producing 25,000 ihp, driving two screws at a maximum speed of 21 knots. *North Dakota*: two Curtis direct-drive turbines, also fired by 14 boilers with similar performance

Maximum range: 6,000 nautical miles at 10 knots

Protection: armored belt: 11 inches thick at the top, tapering to 9 inches on bottom and running three-quarters of the length of the ship; casemate: 10 inches of armor at the bottom, tapering to 8 inches at the top; conning tower: 11½ inches; barbettes: 10 inches at exposed areas and 4 inches at areas covered by other barbettes or superstructure; primary turrets: 12-inch plate protected sides; deck armor: 2 inches thick over vital areas and 1½ inches thick over the rest.

Florida Class Specifications

Dimensions: length: 521 feet 8 inches; beam: 88 feet 3 inches; draft: 28 feet 3 inches

Full displacement: 23,033 tons

Ship's complement: 1,001 men

Armament: ten 12-inch/45-caliber Mark 5 guns; sixteen 5-inch/51-caliber guns (USN 5-inch/51 gun could penetrate 2 inches of armor with a 50-pound shell at 8,000 yards and had an elevation range of -10° to 15°; 240 rounds per gun were carried, and eight to nine rounds could be fired per minute), ten in casemates amidships, four in casemates towards the stern and two towards the bow; two 21-inch underwater torpedo tubes

Machinery: four Parsons direct-drive turbines, fired by 12 Babcock & Wilcox boilers producing 28,000 ihp and driving four screws at a maximum speed of 20¾ knots

Maximum range: 6,720 nautical miles at 10 knots

Protection: almost exactly the same as the Delaware class, the only major difference being that the deck armor was 1½ inches thick across the entire deck.

THE WYOMING CLASS

In July 1908, as the Great White Fleet was halfway into its triumphant circumnavigation of the globe, the US Navy was entering the turbulent throes of a major organizational and doctrinal shift. A group of younger officers, Commanders William Sims and Albert Key being the most vocal among them, were concerned by a number of deficiencies observed in the design and construction of *North Dakota*, most notably the awkward arrangement of the aft primary turrets (Turret 3 could not fire aft if Turret 4 was facing forward, as it could cause blast damage to the sights of Turret 4), the poor location of the engines room and the lack of adequate protection for the secondary batteries. These points of concern were merely a veneer over much graver complaints these officers had regarding the design process of the Navy's dreadnoughts. At the time seven different bureaus, which were headed by high-ranking officers who usually did not have technical expertise in their respective departments, had a say in each new dreadnought design. The Bureau of Construction and Repair in particular was dominated by such officers. The younger reformers wanted a reappraisal of the battleship design selection process that would ensured that officers who both were technically qualified and had sea-going experience would have a prominent role in the design and construction of battleships. It was hoped that such a new supervisory board would push for qualitatively better battleship designs and not settle for ones that were structurally convenient or more politically expedient to build. As a result of the concerns raised by Sims and his colleagues over defects in the Delaware and Florida class designs, Theodore Roosevelt convened a conference at the Naval War College in Newport, Rhode Island beginning on July 22. The short-term results of the 1908 Newport Conference were disappointing to Sims: some of the minor design flaws in the Delaware and Florida classes were remedied, but the overall designs were little altered. In the long term, however, Sims and his colleagues achieved their ultimate goal: in the future the Navy General Board would issue battleship design characteristics and requirements that the various bureaus within the navy would have to meet. This centralized design authority would later be responsible for qualitatively better designs, but two further classes of dreadnoughts would be laid down before this new system went into effect.

The last "big sticks" that Theodore Roosevelt authorized in the waning days of his presidency were the two ships of the Wyoming class. This class was a reactionary design created by the Bureau of Construction and Repair, primarily in response to the Royal Navy upping the ante in the growing worldwide naval arms race. Already in 1908 US naval officers learned that the British were working on a design for a "super-dreadnought" (the Orion class), which would have significantly greater displacement over previous designs and would be armed with new 13½-inch primary guns. This development was discussed at the 1908 Newport Conference, whereupon the Bureau of Construction and Repair was tasked with creating a competitive design. The Bureau of Ordnance had a new 14-inch/45-caliber gun in the design stage and a number of officers wanted this gun used in any new designs, and possibly to replace the 12-inch/45 guns in the Florida class. The problem was whether or not to design a new class of ship around a new gun that had yet to be tested and whether it would be worth the considerable

Stern of *Wyoming* while under construction, showing its four propeller shafts and its aft 5-inch/51 gun position, unique to the ships of the Wyoming and New York classes. (Library of Congress, LC-DIG-ggbain-15883)

delay for these guns to be constructed and tested. Two new designs were prepared that implemented the 14-inch/45 gun (one mounting eight, the other ten), but ultimately the General Board selected an alternative design that mounted twelve 12-inch/50-caliber guns in six twin turrets. The 12-inch/50 gun, which had a higher muzzle velocity over its 12-inch/45 predecessor, was also a new design but one that could be completed and tested much sooner than the 14-inch/45 gun. This may appear to have been a conservative decision at the time, but ballistics experts calculated that a broadside of twelve 12-inch/50 guns carried almost the same weight as ten 14-inch/45 guns.

USS *Wyoming* (BB-32) was laid down in the William Cramp & Sons Shipbuilding Company's yards on February 9, 1910, launched on May 25, 1911 and commissioned on September 25, 1912. USS *Arkansas* (BB-33) was laid down in the New York Shipbuilding Corporation's yards on January 25, 1910, launched on January 14, 1911 and commissioned on September 17, 1912. One pair of superimposed primary turrets was situated fore and two pairs of superimposed turrets were aft of the superstructure. This made for an impressive aft eight-gun broadside and the arrangement of all guns facing aft was a marked improvement over the aft turret arrangement of the Delawares and Floridas. There were still the problems of the location of the engine room between the aft pairs of turrets and the placement of steam pipes around Turrets 3 and 4, but there was little that could be done about the arrangement as the Wyomings were coal burners and thus required the larger coal boiler rooms. They would be the last American dreadnoughts with direct-drive turbine propulsion.

Wyoming Class Specifications
Dimensions: length: 562 feet; beam: 93 feet 2 inches; draft: 28 feet 7 inches
Full displacement: 27,243 tons
Ship's complement: 1,063 men

THE DELAWARE CLASS: USS *DELAWARE*
With a displacement of 20,380 tons and a length of 519 feet, the Delaware class had the appearance of proper dreadnought battleships. The ten 12-inch primary guns were mounted in twin turrets along the centerline, with two turrets forward in a superfiring arrangement and three turrets aft with the third turret mounted on a superfiring barbette nearest amidships. To more evenly distribute the weight of a fifth turret, the designer placed the engine room between the third and fourth turrets. The Delaware class would also be equipped with fourteen 5-inch/50 guns for secondary armament, replacing the ineffective 3-inch/50 guns aboard the South Carolina class. The Delawares were designed with large conning towers with the intention that officers command the ship within them rather than from bridges. This change was the result of a high number of officers being killed on the unprotected bridges of their ships during the battle of Tsushima and all subsequent American dreadnoughts would be equipped with similarly large conning towers. *Delaware* is shown here in its World War I paint scheme.

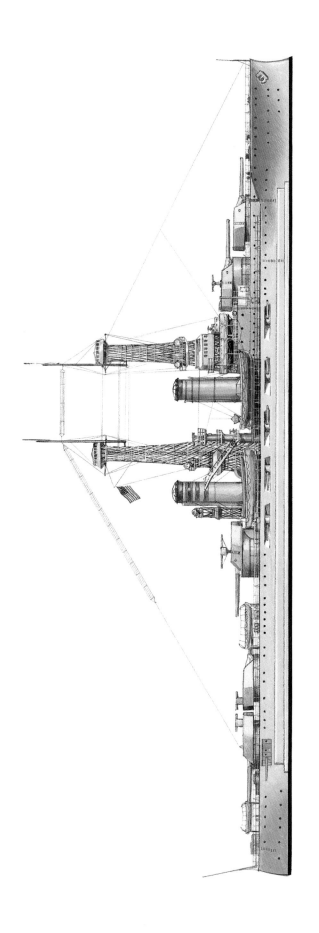
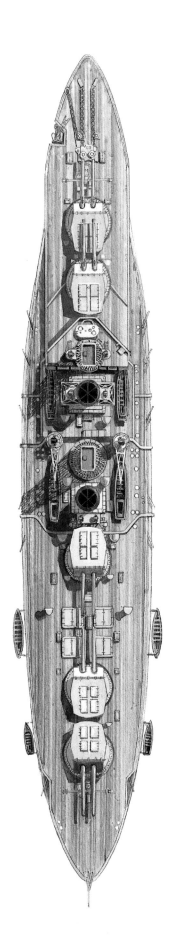

Wyoming photographed from the Brooklyn Bridge after fitting out in the Brooklyn Navy Yard in the autumn of 1912. (Library of Congress, LC-DIG-ggbain-11041)

Excellent view of *Wyoming*'s aft cage mast as it sails out of New York harbor in 1915. The cage mast was a distinctly American naval design feature.

Armament: twelve 12-inch/50-caliber guns mounted in six twin turrets (the USN 12-inch/50 gun had a range at 15° elevation of 23,900 yards, could penetrate $12^{1}/_{3}$ inches of armor at 12,000 yards with a 870-pound armor-piercing shell and had an elevation range of -5° to 15°; 100 rounds were carried per gun and two to three rounds could be fired per minute); twenty-one 5-inch/51-caliber guns, ten were in casemates below the main deck amidships, four in casemates towards the stern, one in a casemate directly in the stern, two towards the bow and finally four guns were mounted in open positions higher up in the superstructure; two submerged 21-inch torpedo tubes

Machinery: four Parsons direct-drive turbines, fired by 12 Babcock & Wilcox boilers producing 28,000 ihp and driving four screws at a maximum speed of 20½ knots

Maximum range: 8,000 nautical miles at 10 knots

Protection: armored belt: 11 inches thick at the top, tapering to 9 inches on bottom and stretching from the fore-most to the aft-most barbettes; lower casemate: 9 inches wide, 11 inches thick at the belt, tapering to 9 inches at the top; upper casemate: 6½ inches; conning tower: 11½ inches; barbettes: 11 inches; turret sides: 12 inches.

THE NEW YORK CLASS

On June 24, 1910, less than six months after the first American dreadnought, USS *Michigan*, was commissioned, the United States Congress authorized the construction of a fifth class of dreadnought battleship, the New York class. The Bureau of Ordnance had successfully tested its 14-inch/45-caliber gun in January and the Navy General Board decided to implement this weapon in the New York class. The ship design selected was one mounting ten 14-inch/45 guns, prepared by the Bureau of Construction and Repair a year earlier, but passed over for the Wyoming class design as the 14-inch/45 gun was still being designed. This design was similar in layout and appearance to the units of the preceding Wyoming class with the exception of having five twin turrets (two fore and three aft) instead of six (two fore and four aft). With three turrets aft the problem of steam pipes from the boiler room surrounding the third turret en route to the engine room still remained. The idea of implementing triple-gun turrets to eliminate the amidships turret was considered (and would be utilized in the following Nevada class), but the General Board felt compelled to accept the already-prepared Bureau of Construction design. Time was of the essence since by the beginning of 1910, Germany's High Seas Fleet had surpassed the US Navy as the second largest navy in the world and Germany had more dreadnoughts under construction than the United States. The General Board, although it was now in a position to dictate the design and technical requirements of new battleships, rationalized that the time required to develop a better design would further widen the numerical disparity between the German and American battle fleets. Thus, it would not be until the Nevada class battleships of 1911 that a number of the critical flaws in previous Bureau of Construction designs would be eliminated by the General Board.

Texas while under construction. The armored belt would be bolted onto the layer of wood visible on the ship's side. (Library of Congress LC-DIG-ggbain-10418)

One major difference between the New York and the Wyoming classes was the installation of vertical triple-expansion engines in the ships of the New York class. This decision was the result of disappointing performance of the turbines in the recently commissioned *North Dakota*. Sea-going tests showed that *North* Dakota's Curtis direct-drive turbines were inefficient at cruising speeds, giving a 45 percent reduction in cruising radius when steaming at 14 knots. There were several reasons for this poor performance that were not evident at the time. First, *North Dakota*'s boilers (and those of every other American dreadnought then in service or under construction) were coal-fired. Coal is less thermally efficient than oil, which ultimately meant less range per ton carried. Second, direct-drive turbines had much higher fuel consumption than geared turbines, as reduction gears allowed a geared turbine to run at a more fuel-efficient rpm, which was faster than the rpm of the propeller shafts. The first marine turbine to be equipped with a reduction gear was not developed until 1909, when Parsons in Britain tested the system in the cargo ship SS *Vespasian*. Given these technical limitations, the Bureau of Construction and Repair was compelled to revert to vertical triple-expansion machinery as American naval planners demanded great range in new battleships. USS *New York* (BB-34) was laid down in the New York Naval Yard on September 11, 1911, launched on October 30, 1912 and commissioned on April 14, 1914. USS *Texas* (BB-35) was laid down in the yards of the Newport News Shipbuilding Company on April 17, 1911, launched on May 18, 1912 and commissioned on March 12, 1914.

New York Class Specifications

Dimensions: length: 573 feet; beam: 95 feet 6 inches; draft: 28 feet 6 inches
Full displacement: 28,367 tons
Ship's complement: 1,042 men
Armament: ten 14-inch/45-caliber guns in five twin turrets (the USN 14-inch/45 gun had a range at 15° elevation of 20,000 yards, could penetrate

$11^9/_{10}$ inches of armor at 12,000 yards with a 1,400-pound armor-piercing shell and had an elevation range of -5° to 15°; 100 rounds were carried per gun and 1.5 rounds could be fired per minute); twenty-one 5-inch/51-caliber secondary guns in the same arrangement as the Wyoming class, except for two secondary batteries in casemates in the bow and only two open-position secondary guns mounted on the superstructure, just below the conning tower; four submerged 21-inch torpedo tubes

Machinery: two vertical triple-expansion engines, coal-fired by 14 Babcock & Wilcox boilers producing up to 28,100 ihp and driving two screws up to a maximum speed of 21 knots

Maximum range: 7,060 nautical miles at 10 knots

Protection: armored belt: 12 inches thick at the top, tapering to 10 inches at the bottom; lower casemate: 11 inches at the bottom, tapering to 9 inches at the top; upper casemate: 6½ inches; conning tower: 12 inches; barbettes: 10–12 inches; turrets: 14 inches on front, 8 inches on the rear, 2 inches on the sides and 4 inches on the top; armored deck: 2 inches.

Breech of the 14-inch/45 gun on the port side of Turret 1 aboard *Texas*. (Author's collection)

US DREADNOUGHT BATTLESHIP OPERATIONS 1914–18

The Veracruz Occupation

The first major military operation conducted by America's new dreadnought battleships was not against an enemy fleet, but rather in the chaos of the Mexican Revolution. Mexico had descended into a civil war of sorts beginning in 1910 and the US Navy began to dispatch squadrons of warships

USS *FLORIDA* AT VERACRUZ

Admiral Fletcher was not shocked when he received orders to occupy the customs house at Veracruz at 8am on April 21. He had been aware of the *Ypiranga* situation and had anticipated landing troops ashore in the event of hostilities. The threat of bombardment from the dreadnoughts' 12-inch guns could probably have quickly resulted in the surrender of the city, but Wilson naively insisted that Huerta was the enemy and that he was acting on behalf of the Mexican people. Fletcher did not want to inflict casualties on the civilian population, but he did not put much stock in his commander-in-chief's belief that the city's population would just sit idly by as foreign troops came ashore. Fletcher and his commanders had already developed a plan for a landing along the Veracruz waterfront on April 13. At a little after 9am, Fletcher put this plan into motion. Each of his dreadnoughts maintained a battalion, made up of sailors (referred to at the time as "Bluejackets"), which consisted of three rifle companies, armed with M1903 Springfield rifles, and an artillery company, armed with a few M1895 Colt-Browning machine guns and a 3-inch Mark 4 landing gun. In addition to the sailor battalion, each battleship had a contingent of marines. Aboard *Prairie* was the 309-man 1st Provisional Battalion of the 2nd Advance Base Regiment of Marines. Shortly after 11am, the marines aboard *Prairie* embarked the ship's whale boats, which were then towed by the ship's motor launches to Pier Four, the main pier at Veracruz and where *Ypiranga* was due to berth. *Prairie*'s boats were followed by the first wave of boatloads of sailors and marines from *Florida* and *Utah*, shown here.

The spartan bridge area on *New York*, typical of early American dreadnoughts. The base of the cage mast is directly behind the helmsman. (Library of Congress, LC-DIG-ggbain-15876)

Stores being brought aboard *New York* on April 24, 1914, prior to the battleship's deployment to Veracruz during the Mexican Revolution. (Library of Congress, LC-DIG-ggbain-16020)

to Mexican ports in order to safeguard American interests and civilians. On the morning of April 9, 1914, a small detail of American sailors were accidentally detained ashore in the port of Tampico by militia troops loyal to President Victoriano Huerta on the pretext that they wandered into a forbidden military zone of the city. The sailors were released, but Admiral Henry Mayo, commander of the American squadron off Tampico, demanded a 21-gun-salute to the American flag as a show of apology. Huerta's government offered a formal apology, but refused the salute. The following day President Woodrow Wilson received a report of the "Tampico Incident" and Huerta's rebuff of Mayo's ultimatum. In the grand scheme of foreign affairs this was a tempest in a teapot, but in Wilson's eyes it was enough of a *casus belli* to take action against Huerta, whom he saw as a ruthless dictator. On April 14, Wilson ordered Vice Admiral Charles J. Badger to sail with the bulk of the Atlantic Fleet to Tampico. Badger immediately sailed from Norfolk with the dreadnought battleships *Arkansas*, *Michigan*, *South Carolina*, the pre-dreadnoughts *Louisiana*, *New Hampshire*, *Vermont* and *New Jersey*, and the cruisers *Tacoma* and *Nashville*. The troopship *Hancock* was also dispatched carrying the First Marine Regiment under the command of Colonel John A. Lejeune. Part of the reason for Wilson's immediate military response was that he had learned on April 18 from the American consul in Veracruz that a German ship, the SS *Ypiranga*, was due into the port on the morning of April 21, bearing a cargo of 200 machine guns and 15 million rounds of ammunition to be delivered to Huerta's forces. Eager to prevent these weapons from reaching Huerta, while at the same time not wanting to violate German sovereignty, Wilson ordered Admiral Frank Fletcher, whose squadron was off Veracruz, to seize control of the customs house in Veracruz and confiscate the weapons once they had been delivered there.

Fletcher's force at Veracruz consisted of the dreadnoughts *Florida* and *Utah* and the auxiliary cruiser/ transport *Prairie*. At 11am he dispatched a detachment of marines and sailors into his ships' boats and sent them to the city's waterfront. By 11.40am, the 787-man landing party, under the command of the *Florida*'s Captain William R. Rush, had climbed up the stone steps along the waterfront and moved into the city to secure the customs house, railroad terminal, rail yard, cable office and power plant. There was an eerie calm as the sailors and marines made their way towards their objectives. The railroad facilities, cable office and power plant were all taken and Captain Rush set up a headquarters in the Terminal Hotel near the railroad station. What Rush's troops didn't know was that they were silently being watched by hundreds of eyes peering down the barrels of Mauser and Winchester rifles. Finally around 12.30pm when a rifle company from the *Florida* approached the customs house a shot rang out suddenly, followed by scores of others. The sailors and marines took cover in the streets and doorways and began to methodically pick off the snipers where they could find them.

The first group of marines and sailors ashore at Veracruz land at Pier Four on April 21, 1914. (Author's collection)

Fortunately for the Americans, the Mexican irregulars were poor shots and the ambush would have been much more severe had it been conducted by regular troops. The *Florida*'s rifle company, under the command of Ensign George Lowry, which was caught near the customs house, managed to silence two machine gun nests and stormed the building, forcing the Mexicans inside to surrender. The Americans' main objective had been secured, but sniper fire was still coming down throughout the city. Admiral Fletcher was quick to respond with help after he received the first reports of what was taking place on the ground. *Florida* trained its 5-inch guns on the Benito Juárez lighthouse across a square from the customs house, where the Mexicans had positioned a small artillery piece and a number of snipers, and knocked out its defenders. Fletcher also dispatched the Sailor Battalion from *Utah* to reinforce Rush's troops. As the sailors from the *Utah* began to arrive in the area around the customs house, the Americans set up machine gun and 3-inch gun positions to cover groups of riflemen going from house to house, eliminating one sniper nest after another. A number of the sailors and marines on the ground were tough veterans who fought in the Boxer Rebellion and the Philippines, and their experience and discipline had a telling effect upon the disorganized Mexican resistance. By 3pm, enemy sniper fire began to die down as most of the perimeter around the customs house was secure and all objectives had been taken.

Throughout the morning hours of April 22, Admiral Badger's force arrived off Veracruz. By 7.30am Fletcher had a full naval brigade ashore, consisting of the 1st Seaman Regiment (57 officers and 1,146 men from the seaman battalions from *Arkansas*, *Florida*, *Utah*, the light cruiser *Chester* and the armored cruiser *San Francisco*), the 2nd Seaman Regiment (64 officers and 1,301 men from *South Carolina* and the pre-dreadnoughts *New Hampshire*, *Vermont* and *New Jersey*), and the 2nd Provisional Regiment, USMC (marines from the *Prairie* and the individual ship detachments). Other units would eventually be formed from Colonel Lejeune's 1st Marine Regiment aboard the troopship *Hancock* and sailors and marines from the dreadnought *Michigan*, which arrived at 6.06am and 8.35am respectively. As American reinforcements landed along the waterfront, the

Members of a "Bluejacket Battalion" caught in a firefight in the streets of Veracruz. This detachment of sailors is manning two M1895 Colt-Browning machine guns. (Author's collection)

sailors and marines ashore began to eliminate the final pockets of resistance in the city. By noon, the entire city had been occupied and the activity of the enemy snipers was slowly curtailed over the next several days. More troops came ashore once Veracruz had been secured, including the 1st Marine Regiment and the 3rd Seaman Regiment made up of sailors from *Michigan*, and the newly arrived *North Dakota* and pre-dreadnoughts *Louisiana* and *Minnesota*. In the midst of the ever-changing events across Mexico, the Wilson administration decided that the United States would occupy and govern Veracruz and on April 27 the American flag was formally raised over the Terminal Hotel before formations of the sailors and marines that went ashore on April 21, assembled in the adjacent square. Later that night four transports carrying a brigade of army regulars under the command of Brigadier General Frederick Funston sailed into the harbor and Fletcher officially turned over control of the city to the Army on April 30. After the transfer ceremony as the ships' marines and sailors marched towards the pier to re-embark aboard their ships, they were given a series of cheers from their Army comrades. American troops remained in Veracruz until November 23, 1914.

World War I

When the United States entered World War I on April 6, 1917, the war at sea had reached a critical stage for the Allies. The British were in the throes of the unprecedented destruction of the renewed German unrestricted U-boat

THE FLORIDA CLASS: USS *UTAH*

The primary difference between the Florida and Delaware classes was that *Florida* and *Utah* were given an improved secondary armament in the form of sixteen 5-inch/51-caliber guns. Designed as an antitorpedo-boat gun, up to nine shells could be fired per minute and the gun's 50-pound armor-piercing shell could penetrate 2 inches of vertical plate at a range of 8,000 yards. It was originally intended that the Florida class would be equipped with 6-inch guns for their secondary armament, but the designers decided to mount the lighter 5-inch/51 guns and use the weight saved for increased armor protection around the secondary gun casemates. The 5-inch/51 gun would be the standard secondary weapon for all subsequent American dreadnought battleships.

Florida and *Utah* were extensively modernized after World War I, having survived the reductions demanded by the 1922 Washington Naval Treaty. *Florida* did not survive the London Naval Treaty of 1930, however. It was decommissioned on February 16, 1931 and scrapped in the Philadelphia Naval Yard the following year. *Utah* was spared the cutter's torch and was disarmed to replace *North Dakota* as a radio-controlled target ship. Re-designated AG-16, it was later converted into an antiaircraft gunnery training ship in 1935. Here *Utah* is shown in an experimental "dazzle" camouflage scheme in which it was painted in 1917–18.

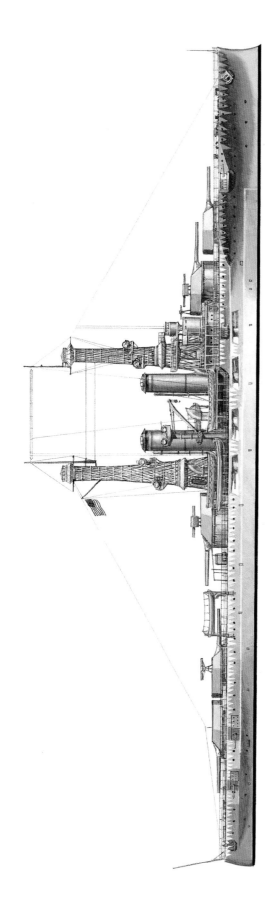
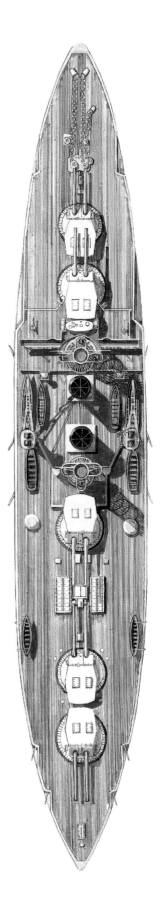

campaign, losing nearly 900,000 tons of shipping in the month of April alone. In the eyes of politicians and the public, it appeared that the mighty Grand Fleet was powerless to destroy either the German surface fleet or its U-boats and this weighed heavily upon Royal Navy's officers and seamen. This was the situation as presented by First Sea Lord John Jellicoe to the American naval attaché, now Rear Admiral William Sims, after the latter had arrived in London to begin cooperative planning following the American entry. A joint convoy strategy was developed that would eventually stem Germany's renewed U-boat offensive, but destroyers and escorts were desperately needed for convoy duty and the US Navy had relatively few ships to spare. The Royal Navy had a number of new destroyers and submarine chasers coming into service, but was short on manpower. Jellicoe told Sims that if the Americans could send him four dreadnought battleships for service in the Grand Fleet, he could lay-up a number of older pre-dreadnoughts and use their crews to man the new smaller vessels. American admirals were reluctant to break up the strength of their main battle fleet, violating Alfred Thayer Mahan's basic principles of fleet concentration, but the internal collapse of Russia, the devastating Italian rout at Caporetto and continuing heavy merchant losses to U-boats necessitated drastic measures. American troops were desperately needed on the ground in Europe and they would have to be safely escorted there. Having finally realized how grave the overall Allied situation was, Admiral William Benson, Chief of Naval Operations, and Josephus Daniels, Secretary of the Navy, finally broke ranks with Mahan's doctrine and agreed to send a squadron of American dreadnoughts to support the Grand Fleet. The ships selected for this task were *Delaware*, *Florida*, *New York* and *Wyoming* of Battleship Division Nine of the Atlantic Fleet, all coal-burners as the British had little precious fuel oil to spare. Under the command of Rear Admiral Hugh Rodman, Battleship Division Nine departed for Great Britain from Hampton Roads on November 25, 1917. On December 7, the four American dreadnoughts sailed into Scapa Flow and were greeted enthusiastically by Admiral Beatty and the sailors of the Grand Fleet. The four dreadnoughts were then formed into the Sixth Battle Squadron of the Grand Fleet with Rodman now under the operational control of Beatty.

The first task Rodman's squadron faced was effectively integrating itself into the Grand Fleet, especially as the Americans had no previous wartime experience. This involved intense and rapid training in British radio codes, signaling and maneuvering and battle methodology. Intensive gunnery practice was also required, as Rodman's crews, who were not accustomed to firing in combat conditions, had initially poor targeting accuracy compared to their British comrades. Finally on February 6, 1918, Rodman's Sixth Battle Squadron was detailed with its first independent mission of the war: escorting Allied and neutral merchantmen along the convoy route between Great Britain and Scandinavia. British battleships had been escorting Scandinavian convoys since January 1918

A striking image of the foremast on *North Dakota* during a training exercise. This gives a good idea of how smoke from coal-burning ships could dramatically interfere with gunnery spotting. (Library of Congress LC-USZ62-7453)

New York leading a line of dreadnoughts in Hampton Roads in 1917. These were the "big sticks" that Theodore Roosevelt had intended to match against the German High Seas Fleet, but American and German dreadnoughts would never meet in combat. (Library of Congress, LC-DIG-hec-08103)

and Admiral Beatty felt Rodman's crews had received enough training to undergo a convoy escort mission. At 9pm on February 6, the Sixth Battle Squadron departed Scapa Flow and rendezvoused with an eastbound convoy at sea on the following morning. After sailing with the convoy to just off the Norwegian coast, Rodman's ships picked up a westbound convoy and escorted it to Britain, arriving back at Scapa Flow at 4am on February 10. The convoy mission went smoothly with the exception of several false U-boat sightings, made by jumpy spotters who mistook dolphins, flotsam and wave crests as periscopes or torpedo wakes. Six days later, the American dreadnoughts sailed with the bulk of the Grand Fleet to support a British battle squadron escorting a Scandinavian convoy. British naval intelligence suspected that German battle cruisers had sailed into the North Sea to intercept the convoy, but it was later realized to be a false report. Nevertheless, this was the first combat mission that the Sixth Battle Squadron had undertaken with the Grand Fleet.

Rodman's ships conducted several other convoy escort missions in March and April, but the only serious threat they encountered was fog and stormy seas. At the other end of the North Sea Admiral Reinhard Scheer of the German Kaiserliche Marine was greatly tempted by a single Allied battle squadron escorting convoys, a target that could be isolated and destroyed before the Grand Fleet could arrive with reinforcements. Rather than send cruisers and destroyers on a light raid, Scheer dispatched the bulk of the High Seas Fleet, which sailed north from the Heligoland Bight in the early hours of April 23. The ensuing operation turned into a comedy of errors for both sides. British naval intelligence failed to discover that the High Seas Fleet had sailed; this would have been disastrous for a convoy and its battle squadron escort had there been one at sea. However, this is where German

Admiral David Beatty, Admiral Hugh Rodman, King George V, the Prince of Wales and Admiral William Sims aboard *New York* during one of the King's visits to the Grand Fleet. Rodman had an affable nature that endeared him to the King and Beatty and this allowed for smooth naval cooperation between the two allies in the North Sea. (Author's collection)

USS *TEXAS*

Texas and *New York* were the last dreadnought battleships in the world to be equipped with vertical triple-expansion engines. It is interesting to note that the dreadnoughts of other navies built up to and during World War I all utilized direct-drive turbines, because their primary intended areas of operations were not far from their ports (e.g. the British Grand Fleet and German High Seas Fleet were focused on North Sea operations, while the navies of France, Italy and Austria-Hungary were focused on Mediterranean operations). Only the United States anticipated potential fleet actions far from home bases, primarily in scenarios against the Imperial Japanese Navy in the waters around the Philippines. The need for long range caused American designers to revert to vertical triple-expansion engines in the New York class, as this was the only coal-fired means of propulsion that could permit long range. The problems facing the first five classes of American dreadnoughts resulting from fuel and machinery would finally be resolved in 1911's Nevada class dreadnoughts, which would be designed with oil-fueled boilers and geared turbine propulsion.

Texas and *New York* each received six Bureau Express oil-fired boilers in their first postwar modernizations, but the reciprocating machinery was retained. These engines proved to be troublesome as time went on. The heavy vibration made it difficult for the ships to maintain a higher cruising speed for an extended length of time. Despite this, both ships served as effective bombardment and antiaircraft platforms throughout World War II. As with *Arkansas*, *New York's* and *Texas's* secondary battery was reduced to six 5-inch/51-caliber guns in the casemated sponsons. Before heading for Iwo Jima in 1945, both ships were armed with ten 3-inch, ten quad 40mm, and 44–48 20mm antiaircraft guns.

KEY

1. Bofors 40mm quad AA gun mount
2. Powder hoist
3. Lower shell hoist
4. Upper shell hoist
5. Turret No. 5
6. Rammer
7. USN 14-inch/45 caliber gun
8. Turret No. 4
9. 12-foot rangfinder
10. Oerlikon 20mm gun mount
11. Vought OS2U Kingfisher observation floatplane
12. Secondary battery control
13. CXAM-1 radar
14. Mk 3 fire control radar
15. Main battery control
16. Forward battle lookout
17. Secondary battle control
18. Navigation bridge
19. 5-inch/51 caliber gun
20. 50-foot motor launch
21. 40-foot motor boat
22. Bureau Express oil-fired boiler
23. Turret No. 3 aircraft catapult
24. Vertical triple expansion steam engine
25. 3-inch/50 caliber AA gun

Children aboard *New York* for a Christmas party in 1916. Admiral Rodman had a similar party for orphaned children in Rosyth, Scotland, when his battleships were stationed there during Christmas of 1917. Rodman and his sailors were excellent ambassadors of American goodwill. (Library of Congress LC-DIG-ggbain-23484)

naval intelligence failed: there was no convoy at sea when the High Seas Fleet reached Norwegian waters. While the Germans were hopelessly searching for Allied ships, the battle cruiser *Moltke* suffered turbine damage due to a lost screw and broke radio silence requesting assistance. This message was intercepted by the British, who then realized that German surface units were in the North Sea in force. Beatty took the Grand Fleet to sea in pursuit of the Germans, who by this point had abandoned their mission; but the High Seas Fleet made it back to within German minefields before British heavy units could close in. Rodman's ships accompanied the Grand Fleet during its pursuit, but this was the closest American dreadnoughts would come to German dreadnoughts during the war.

The April 23–24 sortie of the High Seas Fleet had a major impact on British and American naval planning for the remainder of the war. Although no battle had taken place, the fact that the bulk of the German surface fleet was able to enter the North Sea completely undetected reverberated among the British and American naval commands. If the High Seas Fleet could enter the North Sea undetected, then what was to stop a lone German battle cruiser or small raiding group from sailing undetected up the North Sea and out into the North Atlantic to attack Allied troop convoys bringing desperately needed American soldiers to the Western Front? To ward against this possibility the Royal Navy and US Navy decided to use American pre-dreadnoughts and dreadnoughts as convoy escorts. The first part of this plan called for sending Battleship Division Six, which was made up of the dreadnoughts *Nevada*, *Oklahoma* and *Utah* under the command of Rear Admiral Thomas Rodgers, to Berehaven in southwestern Ireland where they would serve as a search-and-destroy force if a German battle cruiser sailed into the North Atlantic. *Nevada* and *Oklahoma* arrived in Berehaven on August 23, while *Utah* sailed in on September 10.

The second part of the troop convoy defense plan called for American pre-dreadnoughts and armored cruisers to sail as escorts for the convoys themselves. The dreadnoughts *Michigan* and *South Carolina* were also assigned to this duty given their slow maximum speed of 18 knots. *South Carolina* was part of the first battleship-escorted convoy, departing the United States on September 6. During the return journey, *South Carolina* lost its starboard screw on September 17, followed by a breakdown of its port throttle valve on September 20. Four days later, it crept into the Philadelphia naval yard for repairs and saw no further escort duty during the war. A similar fate befell its fellow, *Michigan*, which departed from America on an escort mission on September 30. On October 8, *Michigan* lost its port screw and returned to the United States, and similarly saw no further action in the war. In Berehaven, conditions were rather dull for Admiral Rodger's dreadnoughts as few practice exercises could be undertaken due to a lack of escorting destroyers. There was a burst of excitement in the early hours of October 14, however, when Rodgers received a report that German cruisers had entered the North Atlantic. Two troop convoys were at sea at the time, and Rodgers sailed with *Utah*, *Nevada*, *Oklahoma* and seven destroyers later that day to protect them. Rodger's ships located the convoys, assisted in escorting them and returned to Berehaven on the evening of October 16. Upon his return Rodgers learned that the German cruiser report had been false. The dreadnoughts of Battle Division Six made no further sorties during the war, but remained on station.

Delaware, *Florida*, *New York* and *Wyoming* were not the only American dreadnoughts to see service with the Grand Fleet. *Texas* joined the Sixth Battle Squadron on February 11, 1918, so that Rodman would have five dreadnoughts under his command. This allowed him to refit one ship at a time while still maintaining a full four-ship squadron. Like the other American crews, that of *Texas* would undergo an intense training period in the operational and combat methods of the Grand Fleet. *Arkansas* arrived in Britain on August 29 to replace *Delaware*, Rodman's

Sailors showing off for the camera aboard *Texas* at Scapa Flow in 1918. High-spirited American crews helped to give the Grand Fleet a much-needed morale boost in late 1917 and early 1918 after three years of stagnated conflict (Author's collection)

least effective ship. This now gave the admiral a balanced squadron of two ships with 12-inch guns and two with 14-inch guns, with the *Florida* in reserve. The Sixth Battle Squadron also received a new type of mission in the summer of 1918. Wary of dispatching an isolated battle squadron after the High Seas Fleet's sortie of April 23–24, Beatty no longer regularly dispatched battleships as Scandinavian convoy escorts. On June 30, the Sixth Battle Squadron sailed to cover the first major American mine-laying operation in the North Sea. The laying of a 230-mile-long and 15-mile-wide mine barrage, stretching from the Orkney Islands to the Norwegian coast near Bergen, was advocated by Assistant Secretary of the Navy Franklin D. Roosevelt, who appealed directly to President Wilson for its implementation. Admirals Sims and Rodman were opposed to the project, as it looked to be an ineffective deterrent against U-boats heading for the North Atlantic (it did indeed prove to be ineffective: for over 70,000 mines laid the barrage claimed only six

One of the Wyoming class battleships in the foreground with a Royal Navy battleship to the left and a German dreadnought in the background, steaming to surrender at Scapa Flow on November 21, 1918. (Larry Yungk Collection, courtesy of navsource.org)

Boiler No. 3, one of six oil-fired boilers that provided steam for Texas's reciprocating engines. (Author's collection)

U-boats, and had no effect on deployments) and it would once again put Rodman's dreadnoughts in an isolated position where they could be attacked by a superior German surface force. Nevertheless, for the remainder of the war Rodman's ships would provide cover for mine-laying operations along the North Sea Barrage, with gunnery and fleet exercises interspersed between these missions.

Finally, on October 14, the Americans finally made contact with the enemy, quite literally. Rodman's squadron was sent to sea on October 12 to investigate what turned out to be a false report that major German surface units were at sea. While entering Pentland Firth at 5.42pm on October 14, *New York* was rocked by an impact on the starboard side. Moments later came another blow to stern, strong enough that it broke off two propeller blades. While under repair it appeared that *New York* had been inadvertently rammed on starboard by a shallow-running U-boat, which after the initial impact became caught along the stern of the battleship and struck the starboard propeller, shearing off two blades. The German *UB-113*

D

THE WYOMING CLASS: USS *ARKANSAS*

Arkansas and *Wyoming* were designed with a full flush main deck, something that the previous three dreadnought designs did not have. This allowed the secondary batteries housed in the gun deck, just below the main deck, to be raised by 4 feet, an attempt to deal with the complaints of wetness in the secondary gun positions in previous designs. Regardless, these secondary positions would still be wet when under way; this problem would not be fully rectified by any navy until the postwar relocation of the secondary batteries to turrets or open positions in sponsons on or above the main deck when the threat of attack by aircraft superseded that of torpedo boat attack. This change is exemplified in *Arkansas*'s refits during World War II. In the spring and summer of 1942, *Arkansas* underwent a major refit in which its cage mast was replaced with a tripod and its remaining secondary batteries in the gun deck were removed and plated over. Only six 5-inch/51 guns in the casemated sponsons were retained. It was also equipped with a stronger battery of antiaircraft guns. After its final major refit in the fall of 1944, *Arkansas*'s decks bristled with ten 3-inch, thirty-six 40mm, and twenty-six 20mm antiaircraft guns. Shown here is *Arkansas* in its 1917 configuration and its 1945 configuration.

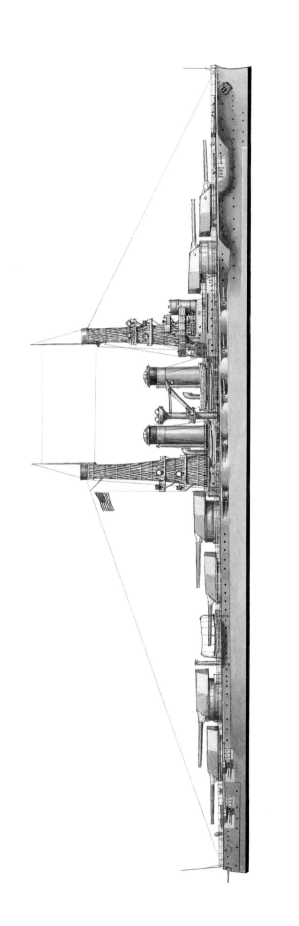

disappeared without a trace in mid-October while sailing in the vicinity, so it seems plausible that this was the U-boat involved. What can be confirmed is that another U-boat spotted *New York* at 1am on October 16 while sailing to Rosyth for repairs and fired three torpedoes, whose wakes were spotted from the battleship, but all three passed ahead. The next time Rodman's sailors spotted the enemy was off the entrance to the Firth of Forth on November 21, the day the bulk of the German High Seas Fleet finally met the entire Grand Fleet, not to do battle but to quietly surrender itself as part of the terms of the November 11 armistice.

INTERWAR SCRAPPING, DISARMAMENT AND MODERNIZATION

Combat at sea during World War I had not claimed a single American dreadnought, but the Washington Naval Treaty of 1922 condemned several to the scrapyards. The Allied powers hoped to prevent another global naval arms race, as this was one of the major catalysts of the last war, and so the battle fleets of the treaty's signatories were restricted to a set total tonnage. As a result, all of the pre-dreadnoughts of Theodore Roosevelt's Great White Fleet were eliminated by the stroke of a pen, as were the US Navy's first two dreadnoughts, *Michigan* and *South Carolina*. The loss of these two ships did not hurt the Navy's battle fleet; their slow speed prevented them from operating effectively with faster dreadnoughts and they spent most of their careers on training cruises. Although not initially earmarked for scrapping, the Navy also deleted the *Delaware* and *North Dakota* from its fleet roster to allow for the addition of the new super-dreadnoughts USS *Colorado* and USS *West Virginia* to the fleet under the treaty's tonnage restrictions. The loss of *Delaware* and *North Dakota* was similarly no strain on the fleet, as neither ship had a particularly outstanding service record. *North Dakota* remained in American waters for the duration of the war because admirals were always concerned about the reliability and inefficiency of its troublesome power plant. *Michigan*, *South Carolina* and *Delaware* were stricken from the Naval Vessel Registry on November 10, 1923 and scrapped in the Philadelphia Naval Yard the following year. *North Dakota* was decommissioned on November 22, 1923, but was disarmed and converted into a radio-controlled target ship. It was finally stricken on January 7, 1931 and sold for scrap later that year.

The Florida, Wyoming and New York classes survived the scrapping of the Washington Naval Treaty and were given top priority for modernization in the mid-1920s. The main aspects of this modernization were their conversion to fuel oil and improved protection. Each of the six ships was fitted out with oil-fired boilers taken from partially completed capital ships that had been scrapped in accordance with the treaty. The ships' propulsion plants operated much more efficiently powered by oil and the smaller size of the oil-fired boilers allowed for more space for oil storage, which in turn greatly extended range. As oil burns cleaner than coal, only a single funnel was required. Antitorpedo bulges (the empty space between the outside of the hull and the outer bulkhead intended to dissipate the explosion of a torpedo warhead) were added to the ships' sides for added protection.

Antisplinter armor was also added to the armored decks. Most of the casemated secondary batteries located below the main deck were relocated to open-top sponsons built on the sides of the main deck. Aft cage masts were also removed and replaced with short stick (*Florida* and *Utah*) or tripod (*Arkansas*, *Wyoming*, *New York* and *Texas*) masts. *New York* and *Texas* had their forward cage masts replaced by large tripod masts. *Wyoming*, re-designated AG-17 in 1931, was converted into a general-purpose training ship, after its side armor, torpedo bulges and primary Turrets 3, 4 and 5 were removed. *Arkansas*, *New York* and *Texas* were retained in full service as active battleships.

Texas sailing into Havana harbor after its first postwar modernization in 1928. The cage masts have been replaced by tripods, but it has yet to receive its aircraft catapult on Turret 3. Cage masts were prone to vibrations from gunfire and rough seas and this had a negative effect on the new rangefinders mounted on top of them. Their structural stability was called into question on January 15, 1918, when *Michigan*'s foremast bent over and collapsed in a heavy swell. (Library of Congress LC-USZC4-14476)

US DREADNOUGHT BATTLESHIP OPERATIONS 1939–45

Neutrality Patrols

When World War II began on September 1, 1939, the core of the Atlantic Squadron of the United States Fleet was the old dreadnoughts *Arkansas*, *New York*, *Texas* and the aircraft carrier *Ranger*. In October 1939, the United States declared the Pan-American security zone, an area that extended from Newfoundland to the southern end of the Caribbean and reached from 350 to 1,200 miles offshore. The first task given to the Atlantic Squadron was the creation of the Neutrality Patrol to detect and observe the movements and actions of belligerent warships operating in the western hemisphere, as well as to protect shipping within the security zone. *Arkansas*, *New York* and *Texas* took part in these patrols for the next two years. Official American neutrality gave way to tacit support for Great Britain in late 1940 as US Navy planners realized that the survival of the British Commonwealth was critical to the defense of the western hemisphere. Already in November 1940, Admiral Harold Stark authored Plan Dog, a war contingency plan recommending immediate offensive action in the Atlantic while remaining on the defensive in the Pacific. Plan Dog was followed by the ABC-1 (American-British-Canadian) Conference of early 1941, which laid the groundwork for future naval cooperation between United States and Royal navies. In the meantime, the British pushed for more active involvement of American battleships in patrolling the Atlantic. Although U-boats were the primary threat to Britain's

The German pocket battleship *Admiral Graf Spee* seen from *Wyoming* during the latter's visit to Kiel in 1937. As in World War I, the US Navy was overly concerned about the possibility of German warships escaping into the Atlantic and raiding British convoys. American dreadnoughts sailed deep into the Atlantic on neutrality patrols to act as a deterrent to German surface raiders in 1941. (Naval History & Heritage Command NH 50268)

seaborne supply lines, the mere threat of Germany's handful of surface raiders caused the Royal Navy a disproportionate concern, which was further reinforced in the minds of American admirals. Successful raiding cruises against convoys made by the battle cruisers *Scharnhorst* and *Gneisenau* and the heavy cruiser *Admiral Hipper* from January to March 1941 intensified the British need for more battleships in the Atlantic for convoy escort duty. Escorting British convoys at sea was too great a breach in neutrality for the American government at this point, but the Roosevelt administration continued to stretch the definition of American neutrality as far as it could. In April, the Atlantic Fleet began to dispatch *Arkansas*, *New York* and *Texas*, along with accompanying destroyers, on three-week patrols out to the 26th meridian. By patrolling the waters south of the Denmark Straits it was hoped that the presence of American battleships would discourage German surface raiders from attempting to break out into the Atlantic.

The new battleship patrols off the Denmark Straits seemed to have little impact upon German surface operations, however, as the German battleship *Bismarck* made its brief sortie into the Atlantic in May 1941. As chance would have it, *Texas* was on patrol in the North Atlantic when the *Bismarck* made its break out of the Denmark Straits after destroying the *Hood*, while *New York*, on its way to relieve *Texas*, narrowly missed coming across the heavy cruiser *Prinz Eugen* after it had parted company with *Bismarck*. While the German warships had orders not to engage American ships, it is uncertain how the *Bismarck* would have reacted if it had happened upon *Texas*. One matter was clear: the old and slow *Texas* would have had a tough fight against the new German battleship if they had been pitted in combat. Another incident in the summer highlighted the Atlantic Fleet's rather embarrassing unpreparedness for all-out war in the Atlantic. On June 20, the U-boat *U-203* located and shadowed *Texas* for several hours, having falsely calculated that the battleship had entered the German war zone. The U-boat's skipper intended to fire on *Texas*, but fortunately for the battleship he was unable to achieve a firing solution. *Texas* had no idea that it was being stalked because American battleships were not yet equipped with ASW gear. The Americans only found out about the incident when Churchill informed Roosevelt after British code breakers decoded the messages between *U-203* and U-boat Command.

In July 1941, *Arkansas* and *New York* participated in one of the more aggressive "defensive" actions made by the US Navy during the last stages of American neutrality. Since May 10, 1940, the British had occupied Iceland after the Germans had invaded Denmark earlier that April, but British troops stationed there were desperately needed on the North African front. Churchill requested Roosevelt that the United States take over the occupation of the island, thus preventing any German attempts to take it. As the

United States Navy prepared to begin escorting convoys within its security zone, recognizing that Iceland would serve as a valuable supply based not only for escorting destroyers but also battleship groups patrolling off the Denmark Straits, Roosevelt agreed, and the terms of the occupation were formalized with the Icelandic government on July 7, 1941. Task Force 19, made up of *Arkansas*, *New York*, two light cruisers and 13 destroyers, had already departed the United States on June 22, escorting six transports carrying the men and equipment of the 1st Marine Brigade. TF19 arrived off Iceland on July 7 and completed the offloading of the marines and their equipment by July 12. The German Kriegsmarine was outraged by this aggressive move, but there was little it could do

Utah capsizing after being struck by two torpedoes dropped by Japanese aircraft at Pearl Harbor on December 7, 1941. Ironically, the old target ship was the first major American warship lost in World War II. (National Archives 80-G-266626)

as Hitler demanded that nothing be done to provoke the United States, especially in light of the planned invasion of the Soviet Union on July 22. *Arkansas*, *New York* and *Texas* continued with their North Atlantic patrols for the next several months and assisted with joint American-British convoy operations that began in the summer. It is ironic that, while Hitler acceded to the United States' belligerent neutrality at sea for over two years in order to keep the Americans out of the European war, it was he who declared war on the United States on December 10, 1941, three days after the Pearl Harbor attack. America's battleships could now assist the British as full allies.

Actions in the European Theater

In the Atlantic, the first shots fired in anger by the old dreadnoughts would not be against the Germans, or even the Italians, but rather the Vichy French. On October 23, 1942, *New York* and *Texas* set sail from Hampton Roads to join Task Force 34, a force of three battleships, five aircraft carriers, seven cruisers and 38 destroyers, which would take part in Operation *Torch*, the Allied invasion of North Africa. TF34 would support the landing of Major General George S. Patton's 35,000-man Western Task Force, assigned to the capture of the port of Casablanca and the airfields surrounding it. The Northern Attack Group (TG 34.8),

New York on escort duty, assembling with a troop convoy in Halifax on May 2, 1942. The old Cunard ocean liner *Aquitania* sits behind the battleship. (Naval History & Heritage Command NH 90210)

consisting of *Texas*, light cruiser *Savannah*, light carriers *Sangamon* and *Chenango*, and nine destroyers, would support the landing of the 9,099-man and 65-light-tank force at Mehdia north of Rabat. The South Attack Group (TG 34.10), containing *New York*, light cruiser *Philadelphia*, light carrier *Santee* and ten destroyers, would support the landing of 6,423 men, 54 light tanks and 54 medium tanks at Safi, over 100 miles southwest of Casablanca. These two landings

would serve as flank protection for the main amphibious assault at Fedala, outside of Casablanca, made up of 18,783 men and 79 light tanks. It was hoped that the French would not resist and would join the Allied cause, but Patton moved carefully if they chose to fight.

The primary objective of the Northern Attack Group was the capture of the concrete airfield at Port Lyautey, a few miles inland from the beaches at Mehdia, which would be necessary for Allied aircraft to use as a base. The beaches at Mehdia and the approach to the Port Lyautey airfield was guarded by the Kasba, an old masonry fort perched above the river. The Kasba supported a small garrison armed with 75mm artillery pieces and several machine guns, but the main threat to the invasion force came from six 138.6mm coastal guns mounted on the same plateau, near the fort. At 5.15am on November 8, troops of the Northern Attack Group went ashore and encountered French defensive fire almost immediately. Surprisingly, the ground force commander refused to consider a preliminary naval bombardment against the French defenses or close-fire support out of fear of friendly fire. Finally in the early afternoon, after taking heavy French fire all morning, an army shore fire control party requested *Texas* to train its guns on a munitions dump near Port Lyautey. For the first time in its history, the 14-inch guns of *Texas* opened fire in anger. For twenty minutes, *Texas* fired 59 shells from a range of 16,500 yards with 20 percent of the shells landing in the target area, destroying one magazine and damaging several other buildings.

Before the French ceasefire on the evening of November 10, *Texas* had one other opportunity to fire its big guns. On that morning, a French truck convoy carrying reinforcements was observed heading towards Port Lyautey from the east and *Texas* was called upon to fire on the road. In two separate bombardments, *Texas* fired 214 rounds of 14-inch shells from 17,000 yards, some of which directly hit the road and destroyed a number of vehicles. No further traffic was observed on the road for the rest of the day, thus demonstrating the effectiveness of naval fire support. *Texas*'s three Vought OS2U Kingfisher floatplanes took an unexpectedly aggressive role in the assault at Mehdia, strafing French trucks on the roads leading out of Port Lyautey on the way back to the coast at the end of their spotting missions. Perhaps the most impressive combat mission flown by *Texas*'s pilots was that of Lt L. R. Chesley, Jr, who was in the cockpit of his Kingfisher on the battleship's catapult when a request for air support was picked up. A column of French tanks and trucks had been spotted heading north out of Rabat towards Port Lyautey. Chesley's Kingfisher was armed with a depth charge that the ship's mechanics had fixed to explode upon impact. Chesley took off from the catapult and headed for the northern Rabat road. In a short time, he came upon the column of Hotchkiss H35 and Renault R35 light tanks. After dropping to 1,000 feet he released his depth charge and dropped it directly onto one of the tanks. The blast destroyed not just the tank that was hit, but blew over two nearby tanks. Unbeknownst at the time, *Texas* and its hard-fighting aircraft had stemmed an armored French counterattack against American troops outside Port Lyautey, who had no antitank weapons.

The operations of the Southern Attack Group off Safi went much more smoothly than those off Mehdia. The primary objective of this group was the capture of Safi and its quay, the only one in Morocco outside of Casablanca with water deep enough to berth the tank carrier *Lakehurst*, which had 54 Sherman tanks aboard. When the French opened fire on two assault ships heading for the quay at 4.28am on November 8, the order was given for *New York* and *Philadelphia* to "play ball." Clearly the ground commander in this sector had no qualms about naval fire support. At 4.36am *New York* commenced firing on Batterie Railleuse, a battery of four 130mm coastal guns 2½ miles north of Safi. After 14 minutes of 14-inch fire, *New York* stopped firing and all was quiet; no further fire was coming from Railleuse, but it was too dark to see if the guns had been knocked out. At 6am, *New York* launched one of its observation aircraft, which later reported that the battery had not been taken out. At 6.40am, Batterie Railleuse opened fire on *New York*, which in turn resumed fire. Finally, one hour 20 minutes and sixty 14-inch shells later, *New York* managed to score a hit on the battery's fire control station, destroying its targeting equipment and effectively neutralizing any further accurate fire from the guns. *New York* had played a key role in protecting the assault on the harbor by tying down the fire of Batterie Railleuse's guns. By 4pm, the harbor front had been secured.

One of *New York*'s Vought OS2U Kingfisher spotter planes landing alongside the battleship after a mission over Safi, Morocco, during Operation *Torch* in November 1942. (Capt Thomas C. Edrington III Collection, courtesy of navsource.org)

Throughout 1943, the most action the old dreadnoughts saw was convoy escort missions or training cruises for midshipmen or gunners. As the buildup for Operation *Overlord* took shape in early 1944, the guns of *Arkansas* and *Texas* would be called upon for shore bombardment duty. Around 4.30am on June 6, 1944, *Arkansas* emerged from the pre-dawn mists, about 7 miles off of the Normandy coast. *Arkansas* was the van of Task Group 129.2, a bombardment force centered around the old dreadnought, the other old dreadnought *Texas*, British light cruisers *Bellona* and *Glasgow*, and French light cruisers *Georges Leygues* and *Montcalm*, all escorted by 12 destroyers and commanded by Rear Admiral Carleton Bryant. H-hour was scheduled for 6.30am on June 6 and Bryant was ordered to conduct a bombardment against pre-assigned defensive positions beginning at 5.50am. The Germans fired first, however, at 5.30am, having watched the Allied armada assembling for around an hour, as several light batteries took aim at *Arkansas*. Finally at 5.50am, *Arkansas* and *Texas* opened fire with their big guns. *Texas*'s primary target was a heavily protected battery of six 155mm guns at Pointe du Hoc, a cliff 3 miles to the west of the center of Omaha Beach. Housed in steel and concrete casemates located in a high position overlooking both Omaha and Utah Beaches, these guns posed the most dangerous threat to not only the troops on the beaches but also the unarmored transports offshore. For 34 minutes, *Texas* fired 255 14-inch shells at Pointe du Hoc and after positive reports from its observation Spitfire its officers believed the battery had been knocked out. But there was a reason why the battery at Pointe du Hoc had remained silent: its guns had been removed and taken a mile inland before the

Landing craft headed for Omaha Beach in the early hours of June 6, 1944, with *Arkansas* firing in the background. (Author's collection)

Allied assault! Sadly, this was only realized after three companies of the 2nd Ranger Battalion had scaled the cliffs of Pointe du Hoc under heavy fire and secured the casemates.

The night of June 6–7 was not exactly restful, as *Texas*'s radar picked up incoming enemy aircraft; a handful of Heinkel He 177 bombers were making an attack on the battleship with radio-guided glide bombs. Fortunately, radio-jamming transmitters installed aboard *Texas* before it left England jammed the signals between the bombs and the aircraft and two bombs came down into the sea several hundred yards away from the battleship. For the next two days, *Arkansas* and *Texas* stayed on station off the beaches, responding to numerous fire support calls. *Arkansas* made an impressive over-the-horizon attack that destroyed a troop train and an overpass on the railway between Cherbourg and Caen, while *Texas* made a similar successful attack against a German troop column inland. At 6.30am on June 9, the two battleships were ordered to retire to Plymouth to refuel and rearm. Their gunfire support had played a critical role in helping American ground troops to secure and exit Omaha Beach.

The next task for *Arkansas* and *Texas* was to support the American assault on Cherbourg. The capture of Cherbourg and its deep-water port was essential for the supply of Allied troops on the ground in France. Admiral Bryant, commanding *Arkansas*, *Texas* and five destroyers (TG 129.2), was tasked with neutralizing a fortification known as Battery Hamburg, located 6 miles east of Cherbourg. Battery Hamburg mounted four Krupp 24cm L/40 K94 guns, which the French had received before the war, salvaged from the old Austro-Hungarian battleship SMS *Monarch*. The guns were protected by steel shields, surrounded by reinforced concrete casemates and manned by well-trained German sailors. While American ground troops were assaulting Cherbourg from its landward side, on June 25 shortly after

G **USS *ARKANSAS* AT OMAHA BEACH**

While *Texas* was pounding Pointe du Hoc, *Arkansas* turned its primary guns against German batteries at Les Moulins and used its 5-inch guns to bombard the exit area at the easternmost end of Omaha. *Texas* later fired its primary guns at defensive positions along a road leading to Vierville, which was the main exit route at the western end of Omaha. *Arkansas* and *Texas* were ordered to direct their fire at the flanks of the beach during the early bombardments out of fear that their primary gunfire might result in friendly losses if used too close to the assault areas; close fire support was left to the escorting destroyers, which sailed much closer to the beach. Several minutes after, H-hour infantry began landing on the beach, but were met by strong machine-gun, mortar and artillery fire. To their horror they realized that the pre-landing aerial bombardment of the beach defenses had been largely ineffective; the bombers had released their payloads too far inland. Fortunately for the troops on the ground, Admiral Bryant realized the difficult situation on the beach and ordered his ships to fire at any German defensive targets that could be located. For the remainder of D-Day *Arkansas* and *Texas* fired at numerous targets of opportunity, located by their observation Spitfires (the spotter planes aboard Bryant's ships had been landed in England and their pilots flew Spitfires on their spotting missions in case they ran into German fighter opposition) or spotters ashore or in the topmast. Here *Arkansas* bombards the German batteries at Les Moulins, overlooking Omaha Beach.

A German 24cm shell from Battery Hamburg landing astern of *Texas* off Cherbourg during the Allied naval bombardment, as seen from *Arkansas*. (National Archives 80-G-244210)

Arkansas off Boston Navy Yard in November 1944 after a major overhaul prior to its deployment to the Pacific. (National Archives 19-N-74312)

noon *Arkansas*'s shore fire control party radioed the ship with a call for heavy gunfire against Battery Hamburg. At 12.08pm *Arkansas* commenced fire at a range of 18,000 yards, but there was no immediate response. Finally at 12.29pm, after the German gun crews had taken their time plotting their target, the guns of Battery Hamburg opened fire. After a while, shells began to straddle *Texas* and continued at an almost regular frequency. Through a combination of reports from its Spitfire spotter plane and observers in the mainmast, *Texas* located the guns of Battery Hamburg and opened fire at 12.39pm. As a result of the almost continual misses from the German guns, Admiral Bryant ordered his destroyers to lay a smoke screen between *Arkansas* and *Texas* and the shore, but the two battleships zigzagged as a strong wind kept blowing the smoke screen off course.

Suddenly at 1.16pm, the bridge of *Texas* was rocked by a blast and then filled with clouds of dense smoke. A 24cm shell had bounced off the top of the armored conning tower and struck one of the support columns of the navigation bridge, exploding upon impact. The explosion ruptured the steel plates in the front of the bridge and sent shrapnel and rivets flying. Almost everyone inside the bridge was wounded; fortunately, the ship's captain was on the starboard bridge wing and escaped relatively unharmed. The captain then ordered all those who were able to get below and continued the bombardment from the protection of the armored conning tower. This was the worst damage *Texas* sustained during the war. *Texas* got a measure of revenge when one of its salvoes made a direct hit on one of Battery Hamburg's guns at 1.35pm. Shortly after 2pm, *Arkansas*'s shore fire control party radioed that Battery Hamburg had been effectively knocked out, which was promptly followed by a message from *Arkansas*'s spotter Spitfire that for a knocked-out gun emplacement it still seemed to be firing quite accurately! *Texas*, despite the damage to its bridge, and *Arkansas* continued their bombardment against Battery Hamburg and their evasive swerving between near misses from the German guns until 3.01pm when the ships were ordered to retire to England. *Arkansas* had expended fifty-eight 12-inch shells and *Texas* fired 206 14-inch shells

for a return of one 24cm German gun destroyed. Despite this rather meager return for such a heavy bombardment, *Arkansas* and *Texas* did play an important, albeit indirect, role in the battle to capture Cherbourg. The Navy's bombardment kept the majority of Cherbourg's artillery preoccupied while the Army took the city, which capitulated on June 29, from the rear. German commanders reported that the bombardment kept many of their batteries pinned down and thus they were unable to turn them on American ground units assaulting from the south. After a brief period of refit and repair in England and Northern Ireland, *Arkansas* and *Texas* were on their way to the Mediterranean to support Operation *Dragoon*, the Allied invasion of southern France. The amphibious assault, which took place along a stretch of beaches around Saint-Tropez and Saint-Raphaël, proceeded much more smoothly than at Normandy. After providing pre-assault bombardments on August 15, *Arkansas* and *Texas* remained on station to offer fire support until the evening of August 17 when the beachheads were fully secured.

Actions in the Pacific Theater

After a period of much-needed overhaul and repairs following their service in the Normandy and Southern France invasions, *Arkansas* and *Texas* sailed from Casco Bay in Maine, ultimately making their way to Tinian in the South Pacific in February 1945. They were eventually joined there by *New York*, which had not seen bombardment action since Operation *Torch*. *New York* had spent 1943 and most of 1944 as a convoy escort and as a training ship for gunners and midshipmen. The guns of the old dreadnoughts were once again being called upon to support a major amphibious assault, Operation *Detachment* or the invasion of Iwo Jima, but this would be the first bombardment in which these ships and crews would experience tenacious enemy aerial resistance. On February 14, 1945, Task Force 54, the Iwo Jima Gunfire and Covering Force (*Arkansas, Texas, Idaho, Nevada, Tennessee,* five cruisers and 16 destroyers) under the command of Rear Admiral Bertram Rodgers, departed for the small island. In the early hours of February 16, TF54 took up stations off Iwo Jima. *New York* arrived a little late, having had to undergo impromptu repairs after it lost a blade off its port screw while en route to Tinian. For the next three days, the old battlewagons fired at prearranged target areas but only when their spotter planes could accurately locate targets. The ship captains were under orders not to expend ammunition unless the guns had a good chance of accurately hitting a target.

At 6.50am on February 19, *Arkansas* and *Texas* (*New York* did not take part in the pre-H-hour bombardment as it was damaged in a collision with a smaller vessel earlier that morning), along with three other battleships, began the heaviest bombardment of the battle in preparation of the Marine landing at H-hour at 9am. From that point on until March 7, *Arkansas, New York* and *Texas* remained on station offshore, moving in and

Wyoming on a training cruise in Chesapeake Bay in 1945. Classified as a training ship in 1931, it was used to train antiaircraft gunners throughout World War II. At the time of this photo, the ship was armed with fourteen 5-inch/38, four 3-inch/50, nine 40mm, one quadruple 1 1/10-inch, and nine 20mm antiaircraft guns. (National Archives, 80-G-323307)

Damage to *New* York's Kingfisher spotter plane and catapult after they were clipped by a kamikaze aircraft off Okinawa on April 14, 1945. (Joseph Zayak Collection, courtesy of navsource.org)

The bow of *Arkansas* today. It rests upside down off Bikini Atoll at a depth of 170 feet and has become an attraction for trained scuba divers. (Courtesy James Lee, Deepscape Photography)

offering fire support when called upon by the marines ashore. Unlike the well-built but visible large concrete coastal artillery emplacements and pillboxes constructed by the Germans in Europe, the Japanese on Iwo Jima had spent almost a year digging tunnels and constructing bunkers, smaller pillboxes and machine gun nests over the entire island. The heavy bombardments devastated the landscape but once the marines went ashore, the Japanese defenders emerged from their tunnels and bunkers to man their surviving defensive positions and take advantage of the cratered landscape for improvised foxholes. The old battlewagons provided more effective service in the role of direct fire support when shore fire control parties could accurately direct their fire against a target. On March 7, the ships finally departed from Iwo Jima and headed for Ulithi Atoll to rearm and resupply. Compared to the operations off North Africa and France, the three weeks they sailed off of Iwo Jima was the longest period of sustained bombardment mission the crews of the dreadnoughts had undertaken. Their last battle would be considerably longer.

The guns of America's last remaining dreadnoughts were called upon one last time for what would be the largest amphibious operation of the Pacific Theater, Operation *Iceberg* or the invasion of Okinawa. Having departed Ulithi Atoll on March 21, *Arkansas*, *New York* and *Texas* assembled with the other ships of TF54, now under the command of veteran bombardment commander Rear Admiral Morton Deyo, off Okinawa on March 25. The old battlewagons unleashed their broadsides against prearranged targets for the next six days, culminating in the pre-landing bombardment in the early hours of April 1, just before the troops stormed the beaches at 8.30am. After this, routine seemed to set in; the battleships would remain on station during the day to answer fire support calls and then retire offshore at night, out of the range of potential enemy shellfire from the island. This was hardly a lazy vigil, however, as over the next several weeks the Japanese unleashed a series of kamikaze attacks against the American ships off Okinawa. There had been some air activity over Iwo Jima, but nothing compared to what the Japanese had prepared for the defense of Okinawa. The first major kamikaze attack took place on April 6, when over 300 suicide planes, escorted by an additional 600 aircraft, struck, sinking seven ships and damaging 22 others. Japanese aircraft had attacked the American ships off Okinawa before this, but not in this number. These attacks forced the antiaircraft

crews of the old dreadnoughts to remain at their stations at all times as the threat of suicidal aerial attack was always present. Crews slept by their guns, had K-rations brought to their stations, occasionally interspersed with a hot meal; they even had to relieve themselves at their posts, emptying their buckets of "bombs" overboard. For as much of an inconvenience all this was, it paid off since the gun crews of *Arkansas*, *New York* and *Texas* were able to ward off or shoot down every kamikaze that dived at their ships. The closest call happened on April 14, when a kamikaze diving on *New York* was hit by its gunners but clipped the observation aircraft and the catapult before crashing into the sea. *Arkansas* and *Texas* provided ground fire support and antiaircraft cover off Okinawa until May 14 when they were ordered to retire and eventually made their way to Leyte in the Philippines. *New York* remained off Okinawa until June 11 when it finally departed for Pearl Harbor after its crew were relieved after being at action stations for 76 consecutive days. The battle for Okinawa was the most difficult for the crews of the old dreadnoughts, but the campaign served as a fitting close in combat activity for the world's oldest dreadnoughts, a testament to their longevity and endurance.

CONCLUSION

After the Japanese surrender on September 2, 1945, *Arkansas*, *New York* and *Texas* each participated in Operation *Magic Carpet*, transporting soldiers and sailors back to the States from overseas. The following year *Arkansas* and *New York* were selected as target ships for Operation *Crossroads*, the atomic bomb tests off the Bikini Atoll in July 1946. *Arkansas* survived the airdropped bomb test (Test "Able") on July 1, but was sunk by the underwater bomb test (Test "Baker") on July 25. *New York* survived both tests and was towed back to Pearl Harbor where it was kept for the next two years to study the effects of radioactivity. It was finally sunk as a target in a gunnery exercise 40 miles off Pearl Harbor on July 8, 1948. *Texas* was formally decommissioned on April 21, 1948, but survives to this day as a museum ship belonging to the State of Texas and is the world's last surviving dreadnought battleship (afloat).

Although experimental ships were designed to meet the German High Seas Fleet in a climactic battle that never came in the Caribbean Sea, the first five classes of American dreadnoughts represented the United States' first steps on its path to becoming the world's naval superpower. Furthermore America's last three dreadnought battleships had unrivaled longevity, serving as effective, mobile bombardment platforms in a second world war, whose course was heavily dictated by amphibious assaults and covered by the heavy guns of old dreadnought battleships.

BIBLIOGRAPHY

Adams, Henry H., et al., *The United States and World Sea Power*, Englewood Cliffs, Prentice Hall, Inc. (1955).

Bonner, Kermit, et al., *USS New York (BB-34): The Old Lady of the Sea*, Paducah, Turner Publishing Company (2002).

Breyer, Siegfried, *Battleships and Battle Cruisers, 1905–1970*, New York, Doubleday & Company Inc. (1973).

Department of the Navy, "USS *Utah*, Report of Pearl Harbor Attack," CINCPAC Action Report Serial 0479 of 15 February, National Archives and Records Administration (1942).

Eisenhower, John S. D., *Intervention: The United States and the Mexican Revolution, 1913–1917*, New York, W. W. Norton & Company (1993).

Feifer, George, *Tennozan: The Battle of Okinawa and the Atomic Bomb*, New York, Ticknor & Fields (1992).

Ferguson, John C., *Historic Battleship Texas: The Last Dreadnought*, Abilene, State House Press (2007).

Friedman, Norman, *U.S. Battleships: An Illustrated Design History*, Annapolis, Naval Institute Press (1985).

—, *U.S. Naval Weapons: Every Gun, Missile, Mine, and Torpedo Used by the U.S. Navy From 1883 to the Present Day*, Annapolis, Naval Institute Press (1982).

Grenville, J. A. S., "Diplomacy and War Plans in the United States, 1890–1917," *Transactions of the Royal Historical Society*, 5th ser., 11 (1961), pp.1–21.

Grey, Randal, ed., *Conway's All the World's Fighting Ships, 1906–1921*, London, Conway Maritime Press Ltd. (1985).

Gibbons, Tony, *The Compete Encyclopedia of Battleships*, New York, Crescent Books (1983).

Herwig, Holger H., *Politics of Frustration: The United States in German Naval Planning, 1889–1941*, Boston, Little, Brown and Company (1976).

Jones, Jerry, *U.S. Battleship Operations in World War I*, Annapolis, Naval Institute Press (1998).

Jones, Vincent, *Operation Torch: Anglo-American Invasion of North Africa*, New York, Ballantine Books Inc. (1972).

Langley, Lester D., *The Banana Wars: An Inner History of American Empire, 1900–1934*, Lexington, The University Press of Kentucky (1983).

McBride, William M., *Technological Change and the United States Navy, 1865–1945*, Baltimore, The Johns Hopkins University Press (2000).

Mehnert, Ute, "German Weltpolitik and the American Two-Front Dilemma: The 'Japanese Peril' in German-American Relations, 1904–1917," *The Journal of American History*, 82/4 (Mar. 1996), pp.1,452–77.

Mooney, James L., ed., *Dictionary of American Naval Fighting Ships*, Washington, DC, Naval Historical Center, Department of the Navy (1991).

Morison, Elting E., *Admiral Sims and the Modern American Navy*, Boston, Houghton Mifflin Company (1942).

Morison, Samuel Eliot, *History of United States Naval Operations in World War II*, Vol I: *The Battle of the Atlantic September 1939–May 1943*, Boston, Little, Brown and Company (1954).

—, *History of United States Naval Operations in World War II*, Vol. II: *Operations in North African Waters October 1942–June 1943*, Boston, Little, Brown and Company (1951).

—, *History of United States Naval Operations in World War II*, Vol. XI: *The Invasion of France and Germany 1944–1945*, Boston, Little, Brown and Company (1957).

—, *History of United States Naval Operations in World War II*, Vol. XIV: *Victory in the Pacific 1945*, Boston, Little, Brown and Company (1960).

Morton, Louis, "War Plan Orange: Evolution of a Strategy," *World Politics*, 11/2 (Jan. 1959), pp.221–50.

Neufeld, William, *Slingshot Warbirds: World War II U.S. Navy Scout-Observation Airmen*, Jefferson, McFarland & Company, Inc., Publishers (2003).

O'Connell, Robert L., *Sacred Vessels: The Cult of the Battleship and the Rise of the U.S. Navy*, Boulder, Westview Press (1991).

O'Gara, Gordon Carpenter, *Theodore Roosevelt and the Rise of the Modern Navy*, New York, Greenwood Press, Publishers (1969).

Reilly, Robin L., *Kamikaze Attacks of World War II: A Complete History of Japanese Suicide Strikes on American Ships, by Aircraft and Other Means*, Jefferson, McFarland & Company, Inc., Publishers (2010).

Rodman, Hugh, Rear Admiral, United States Navy, *Yarns of a Kentucky Admiral*, Indianapolis, The Bobbs-Merrill Company (1928).

Rohwer, Jürgen and Gerhard Hümmelchen, *Chronology of the War at Sea 1939–1945: The Naval History of World War Two*, Annapolis, Naval Institute Press (1992).

Rose, Lisle A., *Power at Sea*, Vol. I: *The Age of Navalism 1890–1918*, Columbia, University of Missouri Press (2007).

Still, Jr., William N., *Crisis at Sea: The United States Navy in European Water in World War I*, Gainsville, University Press of Florida (2006).

Sweetman, Jack, *The Landing at Veracruz: 1914*, Annapolis, United States Naval Institute (1968).

Wimmel, Kenneth, *Theodore Roosevelt and the Great White Fleet: American Sea Power Comes of Age*, London, Brassey's (1998).

Wiper, Steve and Tom Flowers, *Warship Pictorial #4: USS Texas BB-35*, Tucson, Classic Warships Publishing (1999).

Yerxa, Donald A., "The United States Navy in Caribbean Waters during World War I," *Military Affairs*, 51/4 (Oct. 1987), pp.182–87.

INDEX

Page references in **bold** refer to illustrations and captions.